Chromecast User Manual

Supercharge Your Google Chromecast Experience

Learn Everything Most Owners DON'T Know About Their Device!

By
Daniel Forrester
Author & Tech Enthusiast

Table of Contents

Introducing Google Chromecast

Google Chromecast, or simply Chromecast as it is popularly known, is a digital media player developed by Google and made available for purchase in the United States on 24th, July 2013 for $35. A 72 mm (2.83 inch) HDMI device, the Google Chromecast plays video and audio content on an HD television or screen by directly streaming it via a local network or Wi-Fi.

When the device was first introduced last year, it came along with a limited–time promotion program, which offered Netflix free to the users for three months. Via Chromecast, one can easily enjoy their favorite websites, photos, TV shows and, of course, movies and more from popular websites and applications such as Chrome, Google Play, YouTube and Netflix on their TV in HD.

Individuals using Chromecast simply need to select the media to play from the Chromecast supported web apps, mobile apps and other non–apps, or through a beta feature known as "tab casting" that mirrors most of the content on the user's Google Chrome web browser. Chromecast also updates itself automatically to be compatible with a growing number of apps, providing users with up–to–the–minute versions of the Chromecast software.

Over the last year, Chromecast has molded and updated itself to work with the most common devices that most of the users have, such as a Mac or a Windows PC, Android tablets and smartphones, iPads as well as the Chromebook Pixel.

Users can easily browse for what to watch, how and when to watch, adjust the volume on their Chromecast–supported devices, control playback and watch videos in high definition. All from their device, as the content streams on their television!

Under The Hood – Chromecast Specifications

<u>Dimensions</u> (L X W X H) – 72mm x 35mm x 12mm

<u>Weight</u> – 34g

<u>Power</u> – Chromecast is powered through the USB cable (power adapter function and USB cable function both are included in the USB cable), powered either by a nearby outlet *or* the Chromecast's USB port and can be plugged into the TV directly (without plugging the power adapter into the wall).

<u>Video Resolution Maximum Output</u> – 1080 pixels

<u>Output</u> – CEC (Consumer Electronics Control) compatible, HDMI output

<u>Wireless Security</u> – WPA2/WPA, WEP

<u>Wireless Standards</u> – 802.11b/g/n Wi-Fi (802.11n 2.4GHz only)

Google Chromecast supports a wide variety of mobile, PC and tablet operating systems including Chrome OS (Chromebook Pixel on Chrome 28 & higher), Mac OS 10.7

and higher, Windows 7 and higher, iOS 6.0 and higher, and Android 2.3 and higher.

What's in the box?

Google Chromecast device – The device can be plugged into any HDMI (High Definition Multimedia Interface) port on the television, using the existing Wi-Fi network to stream audio and video from the users Chrome browser to the television.

All devices connected to the same existing Wi-Fi network such as PCs, tablets and smartphones can control the Chromecast device, which is powered using the USB cable.

USB power cable – Acting as both the USB cable and the power cable, it provides power to the device. While one end is plugged into either the power supply or a USB port on the television, the other end is plugged into your Chromecast.

Power supply (optional) – Since the USB cable doubles up as the power supply, this power cord is optional. If the television does not have the USB port, then both cables can be used together for their respective functions to power up the Chromecast device.

HDMI extender (optional) – In case the Chromecast device doesn't fit directly into the television, this HDMI extender can be used. While using the HDMI extender, it is supposed to be first connected to the television, and then to the Chromecast device. The HDMI extender could be used to improve the Wi-Fi reception.

Operation

First, you must plug the Chromecast into the HDMI port of a television. Then connect the USB cable to the USB port on the television, or an external power supply.

You'll connect your Chromecast to your home network via your Wi-Fi connection. Chromecast streams video content to the television and works in **two** ways.

The first, primary method makes use of Chromecast–enabled web apps and mobile apps. This method lets you control volume, playback and program selection. The video is then streamed through the device using a local version of Google Chrome. **This allows the device that is controlling Chromecast to be free for other tasks and use applications without disrupting the playback.**

This method supports both the iOS and Android mobile apps as well as web apps which are running through PCs using Google Chrome. (Chromecast-enabled apps include Netflix, Youtube, HBO GO, Hulu Plus, Pandora, and many others which we'll discuss further).

The second method, known as "tab casting", mirrors the content being displayed on a Google Chrome browser that is running on a PC. However, some content uses plug-ins which are not supported and will *not* play easily with the device, such as QuickTime and Silverlight.

Users will notice this when the stream lacks image and sounds. Also, the image and video quality depends on the processing power of the PC. **(Content that is streamed by "tab casting" is *not* hosted on the Chromecast device, and thus may slow the user's computer down a bit).**

In order for the setup and operation of the device to go smoothly, users should make sure they have the following devices ready before purchasing and setting up Chromecast:

- An iOS or an Android tablet, smartphone or phablets, or a Chromebook Pixel, Windows or a Mac PC.

- A secure wireless network which has a network password handy in case you need it.

- An available USB Port on the HDMI–enabled display *or* a power outlet

- A display device with an HDMI input, for example, an HDTV.

Setting up Google Chromecast

This little $35 device from Google turns your TV into a fully functioning multimedia device within minutes. Chromecast streams videos and audio from supported apps such as Netflix and YouTube, and even mirrors the content of your Google Chrome browser window running on your PC or mobile device, straight to the television.

This device thus allows you to turn your own Android or iOS device into an interactive remote control. An inexpensive and intuitive way to stream online media to the HDTV, Chromecast uses the local/home Wi-Fi network and integrates with a number of websites and online content.

Setting up the Chromecast is not just as simple as plugging it in and using the Wi-Fi network. It involves a *slightly* more complicated process of setup. The device setup may vary slightly depending upon whether one uses Chrome on a Chromebook Pixel, Mac or Windows, or whether one uses an Android or iOS device. But overall it's a pretty straightforward setup process.

It's important to understand that you only need to set up your Chromecast device once. Once it is set up, any Google-cast capable devices on the same Wi-Fi network should automatically pick up your Chromecast, so you do not need to repeat each set of the setup instructions for each device.

Plugging Chromecast into the TV

The first step is to plug the Chromecast device into the HDTV and a powered USB port. Users need to remember that depending on the clustering of the HDMI ports on their HDTV, they might need to use the included HDMI cable extender to give the Chromecast more room to fit in properly.

Also, if the users' HDTV does not include a powered USB port, then Chromecast needs to be connected to the power adapter included in the box, which then needs to be plugged into a free power outlet.

Follow the simple steps below to plug in Chromecast properly and correctly:

Plug the male end of the Chromecast device (the HDMI connector) into an HDMI port on your HDTV. If the ports are clustered too tightly, then use the HDMI extension cable and connect one end of it to the HDTV and the other end to the Chromecast device. Alternately, if you want to improve the Wi-Fi reception on your device, then the HDMI extension cable is also very handy in that aspect.

Secondly, attach the micro USB port end of the Chromecast device with the included micro USB cable. Next, connect the other end of the included USB cable to the power adapter, which in turn is to be plugged into the outlet. **Alternately, if your HDTV has a powered USB port, then we'd recommend that users use that port instead of the power adapter as it eliminates all unnecessary cables.**

Once the Chromecast device is plugged into the TV, one should automatically be able to see the Chromecast home screen. If the HDMI input has been selected, then users can read and see the Chromecast setup screen on their HDTV immediately as shown below.

The setup instruction reads:

1) Set me up
2) On your phone or laptop, visit, google.com/Chromecast/setup/
3) My setup name is "ChromecastXXXX"

If the home screen is not visible, then you should switch the input on your HDTV using the Source or Input button on the TV's remote control. You should switch the input to the correct HDMI port and should see the Chromecast home screen.

Downloading the Chromecast App

Chromecast has dedicated Android, Windows, and Mac apps for setup, and they're extremely easy to use. Go to Google's Chromecast setup page on your mobile device or computer and install the app for your platform of choice: https://cast.google.com/chromecast/setup

Setting up Chromecast with Windows PC

Chromecast will only work with Windows 7 versions of PC or higher versions:

First, make sure that your PC is connected to the internet. The next step is to install Google Chrome on your Windows PC, since Chromecast works *only* with a Chrome browser. If your Windows PC does not have a Chrome browser yet, go to: https://www.google.com/intl/en/chrome/browser/. Users should follow the instructions to setup and install the Chrome browser.

Users should then download and install the Chromecast App on their Windows PC by navigating to: https://www.cast.google.com/chromecast/setup.

You should then save the file or run it once it has been downloaded. If you download and save the file then you need to click on the option of "Run" to install the file and complete the Chromecast setup.

After the file has been installed, you can run the Chromecast app. Once the app has been launched, it will immediately begin searching for your Chromecast device on the network. Once the device displays the list of compatible devices, users should select the "Ready to setup ChromecastXXXX" prompt on the screen. You should click the "Continue" button on the installer.

Users should then check the code being shown on their app window as well as on their TV screen. If the codes match, click on the "That's my Code" button. You can then provide the information of your wireless network (username, password) to be used for Chromecast.

Once it is done the first time, the Chromecast device will stay connected to the network. If the Chromecast setup has been successful, users will see the "Ready to cast" prompt on their screens.

Setting Up Chromecast with Android

As mentioned earlier, Android devices are the ideal devices to use with the Chromecast. Since their functionality is well integrated with selected Google apps, including Netflix, Google Play and YouTube, using Chromecast with Android devices is extremely simple.

You should have Android Gingerbread 2.3 or a later version of the OS to run Chromecast. Also, one needs to install the Chromecast extension on their Google Chrome browser. To set up Chromecast using your Android phone or tablet, follow the below mentioned steps:

One should navigate to the website www.google.com/chromecast/setup on their Android tablets or smartphones to install the Chromecast App. Since Google Play is supported by the device, users should press the "Get it on Google Play" button on their device screens to download the Chromecast App. You can then follow the instructions for setting up the app once it has been downloaded onto your device.

After the installation is complete, you can launch the Chromecast App for Android on your devices. The app will immediately search for any Chromecast compatible devices in the range once it has been launched.

Users should then select the Chromecast device they want to set up and follow the setup instructions on the screen to complete the setup of their Chromecast device. If the setup has been successful, users will see the "Ready to cast" prompt on their HDTV screen.

Setting up Chromecast with an iOS Tablet or Phone

Google introduced support for an iOS app to run Chromecast in August last year. Users should install the Chromecast app for iOS in order to set up Chromecast with their iOS devices. The iOS devices must, however, have running iOS version 6 or higher. Users should follow these steps:

Users should install the Chromecast App by navigating to the Chromecast setup page www.google.com/chromecast/setup on their iOS device. This device should be have iOS 6.0 version r a higher version. You can then select the "Available on the Apple App Store" button to download the Chromecast App.

After the app has been downloaded, users should launch the Chromecast iOS App. After the app is launched, it will automatically start searching for Chromecast devices compatible on that particular network.

Once the list of devices is displayed, select the Chromecast device you want to setup from the list and follow the instructions displayed on the screen to complete the setup of your Chromecast device.

Setting up Chromecast using Mac OS X laptop

Chromecast is easy to set up on Mac OS X operating systems. You should have a 10.7 or a higher version OS X version. Users should use the following steps:

First install the Chromecast App on your Mac OS X devices by navigating to the Chromecast website www.google.com/chromecast/setup. Next, users need to drag the downloaded Chromecast app into their Applications folder on the Mac OS X device, and then double click the folder to open it.

Then run the downloaded Chromecast app. Once it has been launched, the Chromecast device will automatically start searching for Chromecast compatible devices on the same network.

Once the list is displayed, users should select the Chromecast device they want to set up their device with and follow the prompt on the screen to complete the setup of their Chromecast.

You can then set up your Chromecast device with the television. If the correct input port isn't chosen, the screen will be blank. Users should use the Input/Source button to switch screens until the Chromecast home screen shows up.

Setting up Chromecast using Chromebook Pixel or Chrome OS

Currently, Chromecast works only with Chromebook Pixel version 28 or higher. Other Chromecast versions for Chromebooks (apart from Pixel) are being developed. Users should follow the below mentioned steps to set up Chromecast using Chromebook Pixel or Chrome OS version 28 or a higher:

Users should get started with Chromecast setup for their Chromebook Pixel or Chrome OS by navigating to www.google.com/chromecast/setup.

After that, you can add the Chromecast extension for Chrome. Once completed, the setup of Chromecast will begin on its own in a New Tab.

Sometimes, the setup might not start automatically or users might want to run the setup later. In this case, users should click on the "Cast extension" button on their PC browsers and select the Options tab. Under the Options tab, they should click on Add Chromecast.

Casting Content via the Chromecast

Casting from your PC or mobile device to your HDTV using Chromecast is the simplest way to use your tablet or your smartphone as a multimedia remote for your TV. Casting is a simple process, and once you're set up to use the device, casting nearly any type of media from your computer is all but a click away.

The supported applications and websites with Google Chromecast are – Revision3, Avia, RealPlayer Cloud, Viki, Plex TV, Vevo, HBOGo, Pandora, Hulu Plus, Google Play Music, Google Play Movies, the Netflix app as well as www.netflix.com, the YouTube app and www.youtube.com, RedBull.TV and BeyondPod.

In December 2013, Google Chromecast announced 10 new apps, and more apps are being integrated with Chrome. Recently, Google announced the development of the SDK app, which allows app creators to install the Chromecast streaming function into any mobile app. Thus, expect many more Chromecast-enabled apps in the future.

Casting from the Chrome web browser

Along with playing media (music, photos and videos) from the Chromecast-supported web and smartphone apps listed above (which we'll take more about in the next section), users can *also* cast media through a beta feature called "tab casting" that can mirror most of the supported content from your Google Chrome web browser. (This essentially lets your view your computer screen on your TV).

In order for the users to cast from Chrome, they should have something called the Google Cast extension installed on their Chrome browsers on their mobile devices or PC. If you haven't already installed it, follow these steps to install the Google Chrome Cast Extension:

Installing the Google Chrome Cast Extension

Users should ensure that they are have the latest version of Chrome. Navigate to the "Settings" tab and click the "About Google Chrome" option. You can then update your Chrome browser, if needed. Users can download the Google Cast extension within the Chrome web store.

Once the Chrome Cast Extension has been installed, you will see a square "Cast" button at the top right hand corner of their Chrome browsers (near your URL address bar).

Also remember that if your device has already been set up, you won't need to reinstall Google Chromecast *app*, but only need to download the Google Chrome Cast *Extension*.

Users should ensure that they are running the Chrome version of 28.0 or higher than that. You can download Chrome at www.google.com/chrome. If you have any sort of trouble regarding Chrome updates, then they should refer to the website www.support.google.com/chrome/answer/95414.

Review the Minimum System Requirements to ensure that your PC and networks are capable of supporting the casting process.

There are two ways in which users can cast videos from their Google Chrome browsers. One is "Casting a Tab", which explains how to cast an entire tab running in Google Chrome onto your TV. "Optimized Playback vs. Casting a Tab" discusses the differences between general web content opened on a tab of Google Chrome versus the cast-optimized and adjusted websites, such as Netflix, HBOGo and YouTube.

Minimum System Requirements

The Google Cast extension is available on all platforms, including Linux, Mac OS X, Windows and Chrome OS, and has no specific hardware requirements. Casting videos from a *tab* however requires specific requirements, listed below.

Operating systems which do not meet these requirements will be limited to projecting slideshows, images and web pages, and will not work well for video streaming content. A strong Wi-Fi connection is also needed for good performance of the videos streaming through Chromecast.

Minimum System Requirements	High Streaming Quality	Standard Streaming Quality
Windows Vista Windows 7 & 8	2nd-generation Core i5 (2GHz+), 3rd–4th–generation Core i5 processor, or equivalent	Core i3 or equivalent

Apple OS X 10.6, 10.7, 10.8	MacBook Pro 2011 or newer, MacBook Air 2012 or newer	MacBook Pro 2010, MacBook Air 2011
Chrome OS	Chromebook Pixel	Coming soon: Samsung Chromebook
Windows XP Linux	Casting a tab not supported at this time	Casting a tab not supported at this time

Casting a tab

Users should follow the below steps in order to start casting a tab from your Chrome Browser:

Make sure that you are on the tab that you would like to project to your TV. You should click the Cast button on your Chrome toolbars at the top right hand side of the Chrome browser.

Now choose the device you want to cast the video to. After a short loading time, the current tab with the video will appear on the users' TV. The Cast icon on your browser will glow and change color to indicate that it is active on the tab being casted.

Additional Notes:

If the Chromecast device is being used currently, then the users will see a short description of what the app is doing. Also, if users wish to terminate the current Chromecast activity, then users should click the "Cast this tab" button and cast the new tab instead.

During the process of tab casting, the audio for the selected video will play only on the users TV and not on their controlling devices. Sounds for other applications continue to play on the controlling device. Users can also switch to other applications or browser tabs while casting, even in full-screen mode using the Alt + Tab or Cmd + Tab feature.

Users can click the Cast icon again while the casting process is still going on to take any of the following actions:

The status area shows what is being cast; clicking on it will return the users to the tab that they started casting from.

The mute button, which is different from the TV's mute button, mutes what's playing on the TV. Users thus need to unmute from Chrome and not the TV.

The "Stop" button stops the casting process. You can also stop the process by closing the tab.

Optimizing Playback vs. Casting A Tab

There are certain websites that have been optimized (adjusted) for the "Cast" to deliver the best possible video and music streaming experience. Currently, there are a number of apps (including 10 new ones that have been launched in the last 2 months) that have been optimized for playback on Google Chromecast.

Websites optimized for playback with Chromecast will have a "Cast" icon at the top right corner of the app. Users should install the Cast Extension to view websites and apps that *do not* support Optimized Playback.

There are a number of benefits of using apps and websites that are **optimized for Cast**, which include the following:

Independent play – Users can shut the lids of their laptops or put their PCs to sleep or on hibernation mode while playing through cast optimized apps and websites. The other option (tab casting) does not allow users to do that and they are required to keep their computers open and on at all times.

PC load and battery lives – Optimized content plays directly on Chromecast, putting no load on PCs and laptops. On the other hand, casting a tab requires a lot of power (as it's hosted on your computer, not the Chromecast device).

Better quality – A full 1080 pixel HD picture ensures the highest possible quality of content for the best viewing on TV through cast-optimized sites. Tab casting limits the viewing capabilities to 720 pixels.

If users are already casting a tab while visiting sites, then cast-optimized apps and sites will usually try to spontaneously switch to an optimized mode of operation from casting a tab. While casting a tab is very convenient for apps and sites that *aren't* optimized and adjusted for playback, users should always use the Cast icon within the video player on a site.

Cast Extension Options

In order to provide users with the best playback experience, the Google Cast extension's settings can be changed. Navigate to your Cast Extension button and select Options. You can then change your settings within the new tab.

These settings are described below:

Auto Resizing – While projecting a tab, this feature resizes the browser to best fit the receiving screen. It keeps the users from having to manually resize their browsers to fit the area that they wish to project to their HDTVs.

Cast to Chrome Quality:

Extreme: Ideal for low interference environments, with high speed PCs on high-speed networks with a 720p high bitrate.

High: Ideal in low interference environments, with high speed PCs on high-speed networks with a 720p high bitrate.

Standard: Ideal for average speed PCs on average speed networks with a 480p high bitrate. Users should refer to the Minimum System Requirements section of the Chromecast user manual for additional details.

Full Screen Zoom

Disabled: Some screen areas may go unused; this feature shows projected content exactly as it appears onscreen.

Enabled: This feature affects content only in full-screen mode and prevents black bars on widescreen video. Users should use this setting only if their laptops have an aspect ratio other than 16:9 (e.g. 16:10, 3:2, etc.).

CPU and GPU requirements

You should know your GPU and CPU configuration and settings in order to determine if your PC meets the Minimum System Requirements for casting.

You can follow the below mentioned steps:

Windows (Vista, 7, and 8):

Based on the Windows version that your PC is running, you should launch the system information page:

On Windows Vista, navigate to the Start menu, then to the Control Panel icon, then to the System and Maintenance tab, and then click on System.

On Windows 7, navigate to the Start menu, navigate to the Computer icon and then click on System Properties.

On Windows 8, navigate to Control Panel, then navigate to System and Security and then click on System. You can also open the Control Panel by pressing the Windows Key + X on the desktop, and then choosing Control Panel.

GPU info can be viewed by clicking on "Windows Experience Index", then navigating to "View and Print", and then looking at "Graphics". CPU info is shown in the line underneath the main system rating.

Mac OS X:

On Mac OS X, users should navigate to the Apple logo on the menu bar, then to "About this Mac", and then click on the "More Info" button. The Graphics and Processor lines indicate the GPU and the CPU requirements.

Chrome OS:

GPU/CPU info for Chrome OS isn't required. The Minimum System Requirements tab has the supported Chrome OS devices.

No Cast Devices Found

One of the most common issues that users face while casting from their Chrome browsers is that they might get the prompt "No Cast Devices Found" on their TV screens. This might be due to one of the following reasons:

- Incomplete or incorrect setup of the device. Users should ensure that their devices are setup properly and test them by casting from their tablets, phones or PCs to their TVs. If setup has been successful, then you should see the name of your Wi-Fi network at the bottom left hand corner of their HDTV home - screens.

- The Chromecast device and the PC might not be on the same Wi-Fi network. Users should ensure that both devices are on the same network.

- The presence of a proxy server or a Virtual Private Network over which the user is trying to connect the devices. Since Chromecast cannot communicate with the PC, tabs or smartphones over these networks, users should disconnect their devices from a Virtual Private Network (VPN) or proxy server.

- The presence of antivirus software or a firewall may stop the users' PC from connecting with the Chromecast device. Users should ensure that any antivirus software or firewall that they may have installed on their PCs isn't interfering with their Chromecast devices.

- Users should try unplugging the Chromecast device, or rebooting their PCs/laptops or wireless router, in case any of the above options do not work.

Troubleshooting On Various Devices

Mac OS X

Users should navigate to System Preferences, then go to the Security tab, and then click on Firewall.

You can navigate to Firewall options, in case Firewall has been enabled. You should disable the "Block all incoming connections" option if it is enabled, then save their settings, reboot their devices and try again.

If the option "Automatically allow signed software to connect" has been enabled, then make sure that there is no entry in the application list for Google Chrome. If the "Automatically allow signed software to connect" isn't enabled, then users should click the "+" button to enable it.

Windows Vista or 7

Users should ensure that their network isn't configured as a Public network. Users should launch and open "Network & Sharing Center" from the Control Panel or by clicking on the Network icon in the Windows system tray.

Users should ideally see their network (usually the name of their Wi-Fi access points) under the "View your active networks" option. However, if you see "Public Network" under their list of networks (with a park bench for an icon), then is likely preventing Google Chrome from linking with their devices. Simply click on the network and check the option of "Home Network" in order to resolve this issue. Users can then completely exit Google Chrome and start it again (reboot it).

Windows 8

Users should turn on the "Sharing" setting, which may cause their TV to not be visible. In order to do this, users should navigate to their Desktop and click on Wi-Fi settings at the bottom right hand sides of their desktop bars. They should then right click on their selected network and then select the option of "Turn sharing on or off", which should be set to "On".

Windows 8.1

Users should turn on the "Find Devices and Content" setting, which allow the TV to now be visible. In order to do this, navigate to the Settings bar on the far right of the Menu bar at the bottom. Then click on "Change PC settings" at the very bottom of the Settings menu, and then select the "Network" option.

You should then right click on their connected Wi-Fi network and select the option of "Find Devices and Content", which should be set to "On". You can learn more about how to change your settings here: http://windows.microsoft.com/en-us/windows-8/turn-sharing-on-or-off.

Users should also know that the tips listed above are only intended to solve *Chromecast setup* issues and might have other consequences. If they are unclear about anything, they should contact their ISP or router manufacturer prior to making any changes.

Casting from Chromecast–Supported Applications

YouTube

To use Chromecast with www.youtube.com, you should have the cast extension installed on to your Chrome browser. Using Chromecast with the YouTube app requires version 4.5.17 or higher on Android or a version of 1.4 or higher on iOS.

Users should follow the simple steps below to cast from the YouTube app to their TV:

Users should search for the video they want to watch and simply press the Cast button for the video to start playing on their TV. On the YouTube website, the Cast button is at the bottom right corner of the player. The Cast button is at the top right hand corner on the YouTube mobile app. Users should then select their Chromecast device from the dropdown menu and wait for their video to start playing on their TV.

One of the main benefits of using Chromecast from any device is that the users can still use their tablet, PC or phone as they normally would while the video is playing. The device controlling Chromecast can be used to navigate, pause, play and control all playback functions. If users want to "cast" the video back to their tablets, PCs and phones, they should simply press the "Cast" button once more and select their tablet, PC or phone from the list of available devices.

Users can also play more than one video back–to–back. All they need to do is select the "Add to TV queue" button on their controlling devices while watching a video. Users can view their TV queue by clicking the YouTube logo, which essentially functions as a back button until you see the TV queue. Any device that is connected to your Wi-Fi network can cast videos and add to the TV queue. Start sharing!

Additional Notes:

As of now, casting from YouTube is supported only from www.youtube.com and the YouTube app only. Casting from an *embedded* YouTube player is not yet supported.

Videos being cast might seem to be low quality at first, but normally switch to the highest quality within a few seconds to minutes. This happens because YouTube uses adaptive bitrate streaming. The video will be downgraded to a lower quality setting if it doesn't buffer at playback speed, which allows for smoother playback of the video. Videos unapproved for mobile playback, live content as well as private videos are not supported for Chromecast streaming.

Google Play

For casting videos from Google Play Movies & TV app, the application is required to have a version of minimum 2.6.9 or higher on Android and a minimum working version of 1.0.1 on iOS. Chromecast can cast videos from Google Play Movies and TV app from the PC, tablet and smartphone to the HDTV.

Users should follow the instruction below to cast videos from Google Play Movies & TV app **using tablets or smartphones**:

Users should first connect their Chromecast and controlling devices to the same Wi-Fi network. They should then open the Google Play Movies & TV app on the controlling device.

Now, select the "My TV Shows" or "My Movies" option and choose the show or the movie that you want to cast to your TV. After that, users should select the "Cast" icon and then select the desired Chromecast device from the device list. Lastly, press the "Touch Play" button on the Google Play Movies & TV app.

Users should follow the instruction below cast videos from the Google Play Movies & TV app **using computers**:

First make sure that you have Google Chrome on your PC. Then, download and Install the "Google Cast" extension from the Google Chrome web store. This has to be done only once for casting to begin.

Be sure to connect the Chromecast device and PC to the same Wi-Fi wireless network. Then navigate to the Google Play Movies website play.google.com/movies.

You can then click on "My TV Shows" or "My Movies" option and choose the desired show or movie and click Play. Then click on the Cast icon on the top right corner of the video player and select your Chromecast device.

Now, you can even continue using your tabs and smartphone while the video is being cast. Select the Cast button on the notification bar at the top of the device to control the video, including using the Rewind, Pause and Play functions. Select the cast button again on the tab or phone if users wish to disconnect the device.

Additional Notes:

If you are using the Google Play Movies & TV app for the first time, visit the app page to learn about the app. Also, remember that at this time, you can only cast videos from the Google Play Movies & TV app that you have purchased or rented. Videos which have been downloaded on other users' devices *cannot* be casted from the app. Lastly, video quality improves as you view the video and the Chromecast can optimize playback efficiently.

Google Play Music App

You can play songs from the Google Play Music app via Android or iOS devices on the Chromecast. In order to do so, the version of the Google Play Music app should be 5.0.11 or higher on Android and 1.1.0.988 or higher on iOS.

Follow the below instructions to cast from the Google Music app to your TV:

If using the Google Play Music app for the first time, users should acquaint themselves and learn more about the app by visiting the app's page. Once you are ready, navigate to the Google Play Music app and select the desired song or playlist. Then press the Cast button in the top right corner of the Google Play Music app and select their desired

Chromecast device. You will see a notification on your TV that your device is connecting to the Chromecast. You music will now play on your TV.

Users can use their tablets and smartphones as controlling devices for the Chromecast. To do so, select the Cast button at the top of the devices. Press the same button to disconnect the device. Users can continue to use those devices to perform other tasks while the music is still playing.

Additional Notes:

- If the battery of the controlling device dies or if the device gets disconnected from the Wi-Fi network, the playlist will stop playing after the current song ends.

- The Google Play Music app is not yet supported to stream local content onto the Chromecast.

- Make sure that your devices have Wi-Fi enabled and are connected to the same Wi-Fi network as the Chromecast.

- Ensure the apps are using latest version. The apps can be updated through the Apple app store and the Google Play Store on respective devices.

- The Google Play Music app for Chromecast is currently only available for Android devices and iOS phones. This app *cannot* be used by your browser or the PC.

Netflix

For the Netflix app to work with Chromecast, ensure the app's version is 2.3.2 or higher on Android devices and 4.2.0 or higher on iOS devices. To start casting from www.netflix.com or the via Netflix app, ensure that the cast extension is installed on your Chrome browser.

Open the Netflix app on your tablet or smartphone and log in to your Netflix account (or go to Netflix.com). If you do not have the Netflix app, you can download it from the Apple App Store or the Google Play Store.

Select the TV show or movie that you want to watch from within the app and press the "Cast" button. The "Cast" button is at the top right hand corner within the Netflix app. On Netflix.com, the "Cast" button is at the bottom right hand corner of the player. Select your Chromecast device and the TV show or the movie will start playing on your TV.

While the video is still playing, you can continue using their tablet and phones to perform other tasks. Selecting the notification bar at the top of the device allows you to control the video using Rewind, Pause, Play, etc. You should press the "Cast" button again to disconnect the tablet or the phone from the Chromecast device.

HBO Go

HBO is fully supported by the Chromecast with the HBOGo app. In order for users to cast from the HBOGo app, the version of the app for Android devices should be 2.3.03.0048 or higher and 2.4.0.2226 higher for iOS devices. Users must ensure that their devices have the cast extension installed on a supporting version of Chrome in order to successfully cast from www.HBOGo.com. Users should follow the steps below:

Launch the HBOGo app on your tablet or phone and log into your HBOGo account. If you do not have the HBOGo app, then you can download it from the Apple App Store or the Google Play Store.

After launching the app, users should select the TV show or movie they wish to watch from within the HBOGo app. They should then press the "Cast" button, which is located at the top right hand corner of the HBOGo app.

Once the list of devices is displayed, select the Chromecast from the list and the TV show or movie will start playing on the TV. In order to use this feature directly from HBOGo.com, users should again press the Cast button within the video player.

Additional Notes:

- While the video is still playing, users can continue using their tablets and phones to perform other tasks. Selecting the notification bar at the top of the device allows the users to control the video using all functions such as Rewind, Pause, Play, etc.

- Users should press the "Cast" button again to disconnect the tab or the phone from their Chromecast device, and select the "This screen" feature to switch playback to that device.

- Users need an HBOGo account in order to stream content.

Hulu Plus

A joint venture of Disney-ABC, 21st Century Fox and Comcast, Hulu is growing in popularity due to growing demand of behind the scenes footage from TBS, ABC, Fox and NBC, as well as clips, trailers, webisodes, movies and TV shows. Hence, Hulu Plus finds itself on the list of Chromecast supported applications.

In order for users to play videos from the Hulu Plus app on their TVs, the app version needs to be 2.9 or higher on Android device and 3.3.1 or higher on iPads and iPhones. Visit the Apple App store or Google Play store to update or download the latest app version.

Users should also know that currently, casting directly from www.hulu.com is not supported by Chromecast. Follow the below instructions in order to watch videos from Hulu Plus on your TV:

Launch the Hulu Plus app on your tablet or phones and log into your Hulu Plus account. Note: you need a Hulu Plus subscription in order to use these services.

After you launch the app, select the TV show or movie you wish to watch from within the Hulu Plus app. You should then find the "Cast" button on the top right hand corner of the app and press it. Select your Chromecast device from the list that pops-up and the content will start playing on your TV.

While the video is still playing, you can continue using your tablet and phone to perform other tasks. Selecting the notification bar at the top of the device allows you to control the video using all functions such as Rewind, Pause, Play, etc.

Press the "Cast" button again to disconnect the tab or the phone from the Chromecast device, and select the "This screen" feature to switch playback to that device.

Additional Chromecast-supported Applications

Pandora

Pandora Internet Radio (or simply known as Pandora) is a streaming Internet radio app supported by Chromecast. Android tablets and smartphones must have a Pandora version of 5.0 or higher to "cast" music. For iOS devices, the Pandora app version should be 5.0 or higher.

Currently, casting with www.pandora.com is not supported. Follow the below steps to listen to Pandora on your TV from your iPad, iPhone, or Android devices:

Users should launch the Pandora app on their devices and log into their Pandora accounts. You can download the app from Apple app store or Google Play store.

Users should then select a radio station that they wish to listen to from within the Pandora app, and should press the cast button next to the volume bar once the music begins playing. After the list of devices is displayed, select a desired Chromecast device. Then the radio station will start playing on your TV.

While the music on Pandora is still playing, users can continue using their tablets or phones to perform other tasks. Selecting the notification bar at the top of the device allows the users to control the video using all functions such as Rewind, Pause, Play, etc.

Users should press the "Cast" button again to disconnect the tab or the phone from their Chromecast device, and select the "This screen" feature to switch playback to that device.

Plex

The popular media streaming device has added support for Plex just recently, and the company has launched a website (www.plex.tv) with direct casting options.

The website is user friendly, features an entirely new interface and is much faster. The sidebar display lists the titles shared with the users and the servers that they are able to access. The Cast button is at the top right of the screen.

Plex offers the options of tons of channels to stream on to the Chromecast. Amongst others, the following popular TV channels are supported by Plex — CNN, CollegeHumor, History Channel, IGN, Khan Academy, The New York Times, MSNBC, The Onion, Reddit, Soundbutt, Spotify, and TED.

Users of Plex TV should follow the below instructions in order to cast videos from Plex on to their TVs using Chromecast:

First, you will need a Plex subscription, also known as PlexPass, in order to stream content using their Chromecast devices. The PlexPass subscription currently costs $29.99 for the entire year or $3.99 per month.

There are generally two possibilities for the users of Plex TV to stream local media content using Plex to their Chromecast devices — either from their mobiles, tablets and smartphone *apps* or from their internet browsers. The functionality of the internet browser is still being tested and the button and function for casting the app is yet to be added.

In order to cast content from the smartphone, users need to download and install the Plex app first. The app is available on Apple App store for iOS devices and the Google Play store for Android devices.

After the app has been downloaded, you can login to your Plex account and select the Chromecast device from the list displayed. Now you simply need to select a video and it will begin casting from your Plex to their TV via the Chromecast.

Real Player

RealPlayer Cloud allows users to watch their cloud videos and local content on their TVs using the Chromecast. RealPlayer uses SurePlayTM technology, ensuring the automatic formatting of the videos being cast from the app to give viewers the highest quality experience possible.

The Real Player Cloud app can be used with the a web browser, as well as Android, iPads and iPhones, all of which have been integrated for Chromecast support. Follow the below instructions in order to start casting videos from RealPlayer Cloud to your TVs.

Launch the Real Player Cloud app on your device and log into the RealPlayer Cloud account. If you do not have the app, you can download it from the Apple app store or Google Play store.

You can then select a song, playlist or video that you wish to cast to your TV. Press the cast button at the top right corner of the screen of the app. After the list of devices is displayed, users should select their desired Chromecast device and the video will automatically start playing on their TV.

You can continue using your tablet or phones to perform other tasks while the video is playing. Selecting the notification bar at the top of the device allows the users to control the video using all functions such as Rewind, Pause, Play, etc. Users should press the "Cast" button again to disconnect the tablet or the phone from their Chromecast device.

Songza

Songza, the free music recommendation and streaming service for Internet users, has recently found support with the Chromecast. The app is popular because users can search for playlists based on not just genres, songs or artists but also eras, interests and themes such as "song in Axe commercial", etc. the app even recommends various songs and playlists based on the users activity, the overall mood and the time of the day.

Follow the below steps in order to cast from Songza to your TV via the Chromecast device:

First, users should launch the Songza app on their devices and log into their Songza account. In case they do not have the app, they can download the app from Apple app store or Google Play store.

Next, should then select a song or a playlist they wish to cast to their TV from within the Songza app. Press the cast button at the top right corner of the screen within the app. After the list of devices is displayed, select the desired Chromecast device and the video will automatically start playing on your TV.

While the videos on Songza app are still playing, users can continue using their tablet or phone normally. Selecting the notification bar at the top of the device allows the users to control the video using functions such as Rewind, Pause, Play, etc. Users should press the "Cast" button again to disconnect the tablet or phone from their Chromecast device.

Avia

The relatively unknown app Avia is the first media player that was supported by the Chromecast. Avia has some great features, including cloud storage, local storage and network storage. With cloud storage, Avia allows users to deliver video and audio media from their Google+, Facebook and DropBox accounts onto their Chromecast.

The local storage feature is Avia's most sought–after feature and strength, which allows the app to scan users' local devices (tabs, smartphones, PCs) for videos, photos and music and cast it to their TVs via Chromecast. The network storage feature allows users to cast content (music, photos, and videos) from a networked computer or server (such as a local media server like a DLNA server) onto their Chromecast.

This feature even allows users to collect content from multiple devices into one library and cast the content. Additionally, Google Drive support is being considered for a future app update.

After you've added all of your storage locations, you're now ready to begin using Avia and Chromecast with your own personal media. Follow the below steps in order to cast media from Avia to your TV via the Chromecast:

First, users should download the Avia app from Apple App store or the Google Play Store. However, as of now, Chromecast support is only available with the paid version of Avia media player. Hence users must upgrade their version of Avia to the Avia Pro version ($2.99) in order to enable Google Chromecast support from within the app itself.

To upgrade, simply press the Chromecast button at the top right of the screen and click on "Buy" on the secondary window that opens up. Now, Avia will refresh with all Chromecast supported features automatically in place. This easy and quick purchase opens up the user's entire media library to be shared in HD.

The next step is to optimize the app's settings in order to minimize any potential errors. Users should navigate to their "Settings" tab, and then click on Wi-Fi to ensure that their device and Chromecast are on the same network. They should then click on the "Advanced settings" option and ensure that Wi-Fi optimization is checked, and also the "Keep Wi-Fi on during sleep" is turned to "Always".

After the app has been downloaded, users should launch the Avia app on their devices. In order to begin casting form their devices, press the Chromecast button at the top right corner of the media player (this button looks like a TV - right next to the settings button). The TV screen will then show the Avia logo followed by a prompt that tells users to start casting.

Users can then navigate to and choose any folder (music, photos or videos) and select any file that they wish to cast using Chromecast. After selecting, the media will begin streaming on the TV screen.

While the video is still playing, users can continue using their tablet or phone to perform other tasks. Selecting any of the options on the notification bar at the bottom of the Avia player allows the users to control the video using all functions such as Rewind, Pause, Play, etc.

To disconnect the tablet or phone from Chromceast, should press the "Cast" button again (selecting the disconnect option). Users can also exit Avia by choosing the "Exit Avia" option on Avia's drop down menu on the top right corner.

Additional Notes

While playing music files, users can choose to enter the Jukebox mode or the DJ mode. Jukebox is similar to YouTube's "Queue" feature, allowing users to add music to a list, while the DJ mode immediately changes the song as soon as a new one is selected.

Viki

The popular Singapore–based video streaming website Viki recently got a Chromecast update. Offering on–demand streaming videos of music, movies and TV shows from around the world, Viki can be used easily with Chromecast for PCs, tablets and smartphones.

Users should follow the below instructions to cast video to their TVs using Chromecast:

First, users need to download and install the Viki app on their devices. Viki is available on Apple app store as well as Google Play store. After downloading, they should launch the app and select the music, movie, or TV show that they want to cast on to their TV.

Next, you will see the Chromecast symbol in the upper right hand corner of the device. Pressing this will prompt you to choose your Chromecast device. The video will then begin streaming on your TV.

Like most other Chromecast supported apps, Viki allows you to use your device as a remote control. While video on the Viki app is still playing, users can continue using their tablets and phones to perform other tasks.

Selecting the notification bar at the top of the device allows the users to control the video using all functions such as Rewind, Pause, Play, etc. They can also control the volume from their phones as well. Users should press the "Cast" button again to disconnect the tab or the phone from their Chromecast device.

Vevo

The video hosting service Vevo offers music videos from two of the big three major record labels, SME and UMG. Vevo's music videos can be watched on the users' TV using Chromecast. The android app of Vevo is even optimized to take advantage of the Chromecast's Lock screen and Notification bar, which can be used as video controls. Users should follow the below steps to cast from Vevo to their TV using Chromecast:

First, download and install the Vevo app on your device. Vevo is available on the Apple store as well as Google Play store. After downloading, launch and open the app and choose the music video that you want to cast on to your TV.

Now, at the top right of the device you will see the symbol for Chromecast, which you should press while the video is playing on your device. (The icon looks like a TV with 4 lines on one corner). Then choose your Chromecast device from the list. Once you choose your device, the music video will then begin casting on your TV.

Like most other Chromecast supported apps, Vevo allows you to use your device as a remote control. While your Vevo video is playing, you can continue to use your tablet or phone to perform other tasks. Selecting the notification bar at the top of the device will allow you to control the video using all functions (Rewind, Pause, Play, etc.). You can also control the volume from your phone as well. Press the "Cast" button again to disconnect the tablet or the phone from your Chromecast.

Revision3

Popularly known as Revision3, Discovery Digital Networks is an internet television network that produces web TV shows an array of topics. Revision3 is now supported by Chromecast and users can cast any videos to their TVs using Revision3 and Chromecast. Users need to follow instructions below to cast video via Revision3:

First, download and install the Revision3 app on your devices. The Revision3 app is available on Apple store as well as Google Play store. Users will also need to install the Chromecast app and the Cast extension onto their devices. After users have downloaded the app, they need to launch the app and choose the video that they want to cast on to their TVs using Chromecast.

At the top right of the device is the symbol for Chromecast, which users need to press while the video is playing on their device (The icon looks like a TV with 4 lines on one corner). Pressing this icon will prompt a list of devices; choose your Chromecast device. Now the video will then begin casting on your TV.

Like most Chromecast supported apps, Revision3 allows your device to function as a remote control. While video on the Revision3 app is still playing, users can continue using their tablet or phone to perform other tasks.

Selecting the notification bar at the top of the device allows the users to control the video using all functions such as Rewind, Pause, Play, etc. They can control the volume from their phones as well. Users should press the "Cast" button again to disconnect the tab or the phone from their Chromecast device.

Casting from Non–Supported Devices and Applications

Kindle Fire

The Kindle Fire is Amazon's flagship tablet and e-book reader, and runs a custom version of Google's Android operating system called Fire OS. Currently, Kindle Fire is an unsupported app on Chromecast.

However, with a few tweaks the Kindle Fire can be used with Chromecast to cast videos to any HDTV. Users should follow the instructions below in order to edit certain settings and allow videos to be cast from Kindle Fire using Chromecast.

Keep in mind, these are instructions for using Chromecast with the <u>Kindle Fire HD 7 inch</u>:

Users should first and foremost understand that the key to casting videos from Kindle Fire is to tweak the settings on Kindle Fire device to allow for third party apps to be installed in their devices.

Next, users should go to the "Settings" tab in their devices, and choose the "Device" option under the tab. They should then select the option of "Allow installation of applications from unknown sources third party applications". This step is done in order to ensure that a certain app called "1 mobile market" can be installed on their devices.

Users should then navigate on their device to the following page: http://www.1mobile.com/app/market/?cid=9 in order to download and install 1mobilemarket.apk on to their Kindle Fire devices.

Once 1mobile market has been installed, the Kindle Fire device basically supports the download of Chromecast supported video apps such as HBOGo, Netflix, YouTube, etc.

Users should then launch the 1mobilemarket and search for any Chromecast supported video app such as YouTube, Google Play Music app, Pandora, or HBOGo and install them according to their specific set of instructions (detailed within this guide). They should then follow these steps for each app to cast them to their TV using Chromecast:

Once the desired app has been installed, all you need to do is open the Chromecast app and sync it with your Kindle Fire devices using the same Wi-Fi network.

Games

Although games and gaming capabilities are not supported officially with Chromecast, the device has huge potential in gaming capabilities.

In order to start playing you will need to download the game onto your desired device. Many games are available for free on both the Google Play and Apple App store. Once you have downloaded the game, users should connect the gaming device and Chromecast to the same Wi-Fi wireless network and open up the game.

ESPN

ESPN, which is not a supported app as of now, can still be view on HDTV via your Chromecast. You can view via ESPNs website espn.go.com/watchespn/.

Follow the below steps to cast the ESPN TV from your device to your TV using Chromecast:

First, users should navigate to the Watch ESPN now website at espn.go.com/watchespn/. When the website opens and the content starts playing, they should right click on the top bar of the chrome window and select the option of "Show as tab". The video now starts playing in a separate tab. You can now make use of the Chromecast button at the top right corner of the Google chrome browser window.

When the new window opens, users should then press the cast button at the top right corner of the window while the video is still playing. After the list of devices is displayed, users should select their desired Chromecast device from the list and ESPN will start playing on their HDTV.

While the video is still playing, users can continue using their PC for other functions by pressing Alt + Tab (or CMD + Tab for Macs) and navigating to other applications or websites.

Amazon Instant Prime Video

Chromecast does not support Amazon Instant Prime Video as of now. Because of this, there are a few issues casting Amazon Prime Video. The channel allows users to cast videos, but not in full screen mode. When going to full screen, the video completely stops on the TV.

Also, the video's audio track is also not sent to the Chromecast and will keep playing from your computer's speakers. Obviously this is not ideal, but it can still be done.

Casting from the Hard Drive

Although not fully supported by Chromecast at the moment, users can directly stream video and audio files stored locally on their PCs and, via Chromecast, watch it on their HDTVs. In order to do so, users should have Google Chrome installed on their PCs as well as the cast extension installed. Once they have finished installing and configuring Chromecast on their PCs, they should proceed as follows:

Users should first launch Google Chrome browser and open a new window/tab by pressing the keys Ctrl + O (or Cmd + T for Mac). A new window will open up.

Users should then go to the File menu and select the Open File option under the tab. When the new window opens, users should then select the file they wish to stream to their HDTV. The locally stored file on their PCs will be opened in the Chrome browser tab.

Users should then press the "Cast" button on the upper right hand corner of their Chrome browser, which is a result of the cast extension file that they installed earlier. After pressing the button, they should select their Chromecast device from the list displayed. Once selected, the video will be cast to the HDTV via the Chrome browser tab!

Additional Notes:

When you are casting the video from your PC's Chrome web browser to the HDTV, you are usually forced to keep the video in full screen mode, thus making it impossible performing any other tasks. However, this can usually be fixed by a simple solution.

Users simply need to hit Alt + Tab command on Windows PCs and select the desktop while streaming a video on your computer in full-screen mode. Mac OS X users will be required to press the Command + Tab option and then select the "Finder" option. Under the "Finder" option, they are supposed to right click the Chrome icon on their dock and select the "Hide" option. Users will now be able to continue streaming videos on their PCs while performing other tasks as well.

- With the launch of the recent SDK app in February 2014, Chromecast has virtually made it harder for users to stream local videos. However, with the help of new applications that have recently added Chromecast support (such as Plex and Avia), users can easily stream local content on their PCs, smartphones and tablets using Chromecast onto their HDTVs.

Advanced Settings, Tips and Tricks

Despite the fact that a growing number of customers are turning to the Chromecast for their multimedia viewing needs, there are still only a handful of applications specifically optimized for the device. Listed below are a few workarounds, tips, tricks and tweaks that enable more content to be delivered to the device. Users can use the following tips to improve their Chromecast experience:

Reduce streaming quality to improve video playback

While Chromecast works best with the apps optimized for playback such as YouTube or Netflix, users might find that videso can be a bit choppy and suffer from buffering interruptions. This happens since the device is dependent on a steady and reliable Internet Wi-Fi connection.

In this case, users should reduce their video playback settings by clicking on Chromecast options in the upper-right-hand corner of their Chrome browsers and selecting the Options tab. There, users need to click on the "Projection Quality" tab and reduce their streaming speeds to Standard (480p). While the video will not look as sharp and the quality will take a hit, playback will be smoother.

Accessing the hidden cast settings

Advanced users might want to check out the hidden settings menu under the Cast extension's Options menu. Here you can find additional streaming settings such as the minimum bit rate, maximum bit rate, frame rate, and other useful settings.

To view these, open the "Options" menu via the Chromecast browser extension, then right-click anywhere and select the "Inspect element" option. In the second window that pops up, users should look for the line that reads "quality == custom", expand that selection and then delete the text "Display: None". Users should then go down seven more lines, and double click and delete the "Display: None" text again, and close the box. They will then be able to see the hidden settings menu.

NOTE:

Many users have suggested that these settings aren't active yet, while others who have said that changing these provided *no visible change* in video quality. **It's best not to mess with these settings unless you are tech-savvy.**

Using PC/laptop while streaming video content

One of the biggest advantages of using the Chromecast device from PCs and mobile devices is its ability to multitask. Users can cast videos from their PCs and mobile devices to their TVs, while at the same time use other applications normally.

However, users need to be sure to keep the video content in full screen mode when they are casting videos from their PC's web browser. Once in full-screen mode, simply press keys Alt + Tab and select the Desktop while streaming videos in full screen mode (for Windows users).

Mac users should select the Command + Tab keys, then navigate to the Finder tab. They should then go to the Chrome icon on their dock and right click on it to select Hide. Users will then be able to perform other tasks on their Macs.

Mirroring PC display on the HDTV

Users can mirror their PC's *entire* desktop. Simply open the Chrome extensions on your Chrome web browsers and click on the Cast in the top right hand corner. Then click on the drop down arrow and select the "Cast Entire Screen (experimental)" option.

Note that this option could be unstable and is considered experimental. Also, sound will come from the PC's speakers, not the TVs. However, it is still a good option for sharing photo slideshows or viewing PowerPoint presentations.

Streaming Audio from Audio Players and Programs

While full-screen sharing is simple to use, the feature, as of now, does not support audio streaming and sharing. Howver, users can navigate around the feature and use the "Remote Desktop Web app" for the same.

You can open the computer you're currently using as a tab within the Remote Desktop app. Once you've set up Remote Desktop (see the Remote Desktop section on Google Chromecast's website here: https://support.google.com/chrome/answer/1649523?hl =en), users should open the app and from the My Computer list select their current computer.

Ensure that the audio is turned off on their PCs, or the music will start playing on both devices at the same time.

Using the *TeamViewer* app as a makeshift remote

TeamViewer allows users to cast videos from their Google Chrome browser on their PCs to the Chromecast device. The TeamViewer app acts as a remote control for the PC, so once the video is up and running, users can exit the app and keep running other activities on their device. Just make sure to turn your PC's audio off before you start casting, or the music will start playing on both devices at the same time.

Rooting Chromecast

Users will need the following in order to root their Chromecast devices: a Chromecast, a Powered Micro USB OTG cable, a USB Flash Drive with minimum storage capacity of 128MB, the Exploit Package (which can be downloaded from the Bootloader Exploit Package – available online), the device driver file (DD file) and about 12 minutes to go through the entire process.

In order to root Chromecast, follow the instructions below:

Before you begin: Users should know that rooting the Chromecast will void the warranty. You can then download both the Exploit Package file and the DD (device driver) file and place both the files as well as all supported content on the desktop (you can find these online, including http://gtvhacker.com/index.php/Google_Chromecast - as well as some other sites).

Users should then extract both the setup files from both the archives and place them both on the desktop. You can then plug in your USB Flash drives (with 128MB+ storage spaces) to your PCs and launch a Command Prompt Window on your Desktop (by holding Shift and right clicking anywhere on the desktop). Next choose the "Open Command Window here" option.

Users should then type in the following command – "dd if=gtvhacker-chromecast.bin of=/dev/sdXbs=1024" – into the Command Prompt Window.
Next, plug the USB flash drive into one end of Chromecast and plug the other end into the USB OTG cable. They should then press and hold the button on the Chromecast device while connecting it to the power cord and outlet.

Once the above steps are completed, the Chromecast will automatically complete the rest of the steps to gain root-access. Once root access is gained, users can then use the device for a variety of applications.

*Please note: rooting should only be attempted by **tech-savvy, advanced users**!*

Travelling With Chromecast

Since Chromecast is small in size and portable, many potential buyers are considering buying it because they think they can use it in hotels. The problem with Chromecast is it only works with Wi-Fi internet access, and thus, either works or is non-functional.

Even though most hotels today have solid Wi-Fi for their guests, most of them disable any peer-to-peer communication on their networks. Moreover, the device does not currently have any support for captive wireless networks. (Captive networks are those networks that require users to log in through browsers before accessing the web).

Although users could set up personal hotspots through their smartphones or PCs, the data usage charges alone may make using the Chromecast impractical.
Another workaround is for users to bring their own travel-size access point and plug it into the hotel's Ethernet port. PC applications such as Connectify could also create

hotspots on the users' PCs, which *may* make using the Chromecast possible.

Chromecast FAQs

What is HDMI? (High Definition Multimedia Interface)

HDMI stands for High Definition Multimedia Interface, which is common in new-age television set nowadays. The Chromecast device needs a display device that possesses an HDMI input. The Chromecast box contains an HDMI extension cable, which can be used if the Chromecast doesn't directly fit into the TV due to the positioning of the HDMI port. Otherwise, the HDMI cable is not required.

What is CEC? (Consumer Electronics Control)

CEC or Consumer Electronics Control allows users to control all their HDMI devices with one single remote control. For example, if the users' TV set has CEC support, then they may be able to turn on and change the input on their HDTV using just their tablet, smartphone or PC. *However, the Chromecast device must be powered by a power outlet in order for CEC to work.*

CECs are known by different names by different manufacturers. These include: NetCommand for HDMI

(Mitsubishi), EasyLink (Philips), VIERA Link (Panasonic), EZ-Sync, HDAVI Control, SimpLink (LG), CE-Link and Regza Link (Toshiba), HDMI-CEC (Hitachi), BRAVIA Link and BRAVIA Sync (Sony), Aquos Link (Sharp), and Anynet+ (Samsung).

Moving Chromecast device to a new TV

The Chromecast's size makes it very portable. Users can move it easily from one room to another and use it with various HDMI supported displays. The best part is that users do not need to set up the Chromecast if it's linked to the *same* Wi-Fi network as it was connected to earlier.

Performing Factory Data Reset (FDR) on the device

There are two ways for users to perform a data reset (FDR or a Factory Data Reset) on their Chromecast devices:

Performing FDR on the device using Chromecast app – Users will locate the option to do a data reset under the "Menu" or "settings" options on the app, or.

Secondly, users can simply press and hold the button on their Chromecast device until the solid red light (see LED lights FAQ) starts flashing.

Changing the Wi-Fi network or wireless settings on the already set up Chromecast device.

If users wish to change their Wi-Fi networks that their Chromecast device is linked to, they either need to perform a FDR (Factory Data Reset) or they could use the following steps:

- Power on Chromecast – In order to change the Wi-Fi network on the Chromecast device, the device must be connected to any home Wi-Fi network. Users should then link their viewing devices (either tablet, smartphone, or PC) to the same Wi-Fi network and power them on in order to perform the changes.

- Launch the Chromecast App – Users will need to open the Chromecast app on their devices in order to manage the Wi–Fi network for Chromecast devices. The device (tablet, smartphone or laptop) will begin searching for Chromecast devices on the same network or in the same range.

- Connect Chromecast to mobile device – Users should then connect their devices to the Chromecast by tapping on the Chromecast device name in the devices page. Once the Chromecast device has been connected to the same network as the controlling device, it is now ready for setup.

Change Chromecast Wi–Fi network – In order to change the Wi-Fi network on the Chromecast device, users should simply tap the network entry on their controlling device. A popup window will open showcasing the current network information. Users should then tap on the Wi-Fi network that they are using, which will get them the list of Wi-Fi networks in range (discovered by their Chromecast device). They should then tap on the *new* Wi-Fi network that they want to use. After providing the password for that new Wi-Fi network, users should click on "OK" to successfully change the Chromecast Wi-Fi network.

Warning message – This set of actions may prompt the device to send users a warning message notifying them that their controlling device will not be on the same network as their Chromecast. However, users needn't worry because as soon as they change the Chromecast's Wi-Fi network, the device automatically switches the controlling device's Wi-Fi network to the same network as the Chromecast. However, the password of the new network needs to have been saved on the controlling devices or the connection may fail.

Using Chromecast and the casting process in Chrome incognito mode

Users can use the casting process even when chrome is in the incognito mode. In order to do so, users need to type chrome://extensions into their browser bars, search for and find the Google Cast extension, and select the "Enable in incognito" option.

Naming and renaming Chromecast devices

Users have the option of naming their Chromecast device during the setup process. They can also rename the Chromecast device at a later stage from the Chromecast setup app.

Casting with two separate compatible apps and devices to the HDTV at the same time

Multiple users can cast to the HDTV if they are both on the same Wi-Fi network and they are both using applications that are supported for Cast. Users should ensure the safety of their network and devices by requiring a username and password.

Chromecast router compatibility

Google has identified a list of specific routers that work well out-of-the-box with the Chromecast. Keep in mind that making any sort of changes to the router settings might make it incompatible with the Chromecast.

Users should consult their ISP or router manufacturer if they are facing any problems or they have any doubts, questions or concerns. The list of supported routers is available at the following page on Google's website: https://support.google.com/chromecast/table/3477832?hl=en&ref_topic=3447927

Using Chromecast outside the United States

Chromecast can be outside the U.S. with certain applications, but region–aware apps like Hulu and Netflix will require using a separate DNS if the app is not supported by the user's region.

More than one Chromecast on the same network

Users can use more than one Chromecast on the same Wi-Fi network. They will appear listed under their respective names when users initiate a cast.

Google Play Movies credit with Chromecast

Early buyers of Chromecast may have a $6 Google Play Movies credit with their Chromecast device. This $6 credit can be used via the Google Wallet app. Users can buy any content, other than subscriptions, Google Play Store. However, this is valid only till 31st March 2014, thus users should redeem their codes before that date.

Wireless network details

Chromecast supports 2.4 GHz 802.11 b/g/ according to the Google Play Store specifications. Users should not connect their devices through the 802.11b network unless they have no other devices using this frequency, or they have zero signal interference.

LED status indicators for Chromecast

Solid red – Indicates the start-up process (the light should go white afterwards) and in during settings reset process (by continuously holding the button down).

Solid white – This means that Chromecast device has been connected to a Wi–Fi network.

<u>Blinking white</u> – This means that the Chromecast device is *not* connected to a Wi–Fi network.

Advantages of Google Chromecast

Ultimately you will be the judge, but we think the advantages of Google's $35 portable device outweigh its disadvantages!

- Google Chromecast is an simple, intuitive way to watch video from the internet on your TV (in HD).

- Many of the Chromecast's supported applications act as remote controls themselves *instead* of using traditional remote controls. These apps allow users to choose what to watch at the press of a button.

- Users can use the controlling devices to perform other activities while the video is still streaming on their TV, eliminating the need for separate devices while streaming.

- Users can use the controlling device to play, pause, rewind, as well as turn the volume up or down, without using the television remote.

- Chromecast is well supported, integrating with both iOS and Android devices.

- Google Chromecast works extremely well with the supported apps, allowing for full screen playing, and also works great with music services such as Pandora and Rdio. Audio files with the MP3 format and videos with the MP4 format work great as well.